How to use these notes

Guided Reading

Walkthrough/Book introduction (pages 2–3)

A *walkthrough*, or book introduction, is a way of introducing the book to a group of children. During the walkthrough, children are introduced to some of the ideas and significant vocabulary they will meet when they read the book.

Go through the whole of the walkthrough before the children start reading independently. The walkthrough notes on pages 2 and 3 of this booklet provide prompts for you to use, specific to *Rescue!* The questions, comments and suggestions alert children to ideas and vocabulary they will need in order to read independently and with full understanding.

Independent Reading (pages 4–5)

After doing a walkthrough, ask the children to read the text aloud, on their own, at their own pace. Observe the strategies each child uses, praising successful problem solving and expressive reading. Prompts are suggested for good phrasing, use of word-solving skills, predicting and checking the meaning, and actively monitoring the implications of the text, on pages 4 and 5.

After Independent Reading/ Returning to the text (page 6)

After the children have read the book independently, return to the text as a group to reinforce teaching points and to check children's understanding. On page 6, there are quick follow-up ideas for related text, sentence and word level work.

Responding to the text (pages 6–8)

It is important to encourage children to give a personal response to the text. Discussion ideas related to the book are on page 6.

These Teaching Notes also contain group activity ideas on page 7, and a Photocopy Master on page 8, for use after the guided reading session or in a follow-up literacy session.

Guided Reading Notes

Walkthrough

Ask the children to read the title and the back cover blurb. What sort of story do they think this is going to be? Bring the children back to the story by asking them to read the title again on the title page.

Pages 2–3

PROMPTS What are the boys in the picture doing? What do you think might happen to Tom?

Pages 4–5

PROMPTS Were you right? What will Tom's Mum and Dad do to help? Yes, Mum's going to phone for the coastguard. (Help the children to locate *coastguard* on page 5.) What do you notice about how this story is told? (Prompt for *speech bubbles*.)

Walk through to page 10 with the children, asking them to describe the action in the pictures, and to predict what will happen as they go along.

Pages 10–11

PROMPTS At last, the coastguard and the rescue boat have arrived! How are they going to rescue Tom and his dad? Yes, they're going to send a diver down to the cave with a rope.

Walk through to page 14 with the children, talking about the pictures.

Pages 14–15

PROMPTS How do you think Tom and his dad feel now that they're back in the lifeboat? Can you find *lifeboat* in the text?

Finish the walkthrough by discussing how all the speech is shown in speech bubbles. Remind the children to read them from left to right when they are reading independently.

Independent Reading

Before the children start to read independently, remind them of the strategies they can use to help them read unfamiliar words. These could include: using print information, finding clues in the pictures, predicting the meaning of the word from its context, applying their understanding of grammar, etc.

Pages 4–5

CHECK for accurate reading of *coastguard*.

> "Who came to rescue Tom and Dad? It was the coastguard, wasn't it? Can you see two smaller words there?"

CHECK that the child reads the speech bubbles in the right order.

Pages 6–7

CHECK that the child uses knowledge of initial consonant clusters to read *plunged* and *dragged* and pronounces the final *d* clearly.

Ask the child to read on, checking that he or she reads the text in the speech bubbles after the narrative.

Pages 10–11

█ CHECK █ for accurate reading of *rescue*.

"What is this book called? Does that word look like the word on the cover?"

Ask the child to read on, checking that he or she is reading the dialogue expressively.

Pages 14–15

█ CHECK █ for accurate reading of *lifeboat*.

"Can you remember the special name for the rescue boat? Try splitting the word into two smaller words."

Word knowledge – use word endings to support reading

Ask the children to look through the book and find the past tense of these words: *wash* (page 3), *scream* (page 4), *plunge* (page 6), *drag* (page 6) and *suck* (page 6).

What do all the words end with? Ask the children to find a verb in the past tense on page 10 that does not end with *ed* (*came*, *knew*).

Extend this to other words in the text: *fish*, *see*, *stay*, *phone*, *send*, *know*.

Sentence knowledge – use words and phrases that link sentences

Ask the children to reread page 14. Can they find the phrase that links the first sentence to the previous page? Prompt for *At last*. Ask the children to think of other phrases that link sentences showing how time moves on (like *Meanwhile*, *After a while*, *Next*).

Text knowledge – link familiar story themes to own experiences

How do the children think each character felt when Tom was swept into the sea? How would the children themselves have felt? Talk about children's own experiences at the seaside, for instance, looking in rock pools, playing in the sea, being knocked over by waves or feeling the sea tugging at their legs.

Responding to the text

- Ask the children what caused Tom to fall in the sea.
- How did Jamie help?
- Who was brave in the story?
- Did all the characters do the right thing? Should anyone have behaved differently?

➊ Speech bubbles

AIM to investigate ways of presenting texts *(NLS: Y2 T2 S7)*

YOU WILL NEED
● flip chart
● marker pens
● some stories with lots of dialogue

WHAT TO DO Look again at the way the speech in the story is presented. Draw a speech bubble on the flip chart, and write in some speech from the story. Ask the children to locate some dialogue in one of their reading books, and help them to decide which words would go into the speech bubble. Help children to recognize actual spoken words by writing a short conversation in speech bubbles.

➋ Reading aloud

AIM to read aloud with expression and intonation, appropriate to the punctuation *(NLS: Y2 T2 S2)*

YOU WILL NEED ● copies of *Rescue!*

WHAT TO DO Ask the children what they should do when they encounter the following punctuation: a comma (*pause for a moment*), a full stop (*pause for a little longer*), an exclamation mark (*speak with emphasis to suggest surprise, a sense of danger, etc*) and a question mark (*raise their voice a bit at the end of the sentence*). Ask a child to read pages 4 and 5 in a flat voice, ignoring all the punctuation. Now read pages 4 and 5 yourself, putting the punctuation in the wrong places. Discuss what effect this has on their understanding and enjoyment.

Changing the tense

1 Tom and Jamie _____
   fishing in the rock pools.

2 Jamie _____ the huge
   wave coming.

3 The wave _____ Tom
   over the edge of the rock.

4 Tom _____ in the sea.

5 Tom's dad _____ in
   the sea.

6 The diver _____ through
   the gap into the cave.

7 Dad _____ Tom into the
   harness.

8 The boat _____ them safely
   back to Mum.

are/were

saw/see

washed/washes

falls/fell

plunged/plunges

swims/swam

helps/helped

takes/took

Ask the children to complete the sentences by choosing the right word. Encourage them to read the sentences and think about which word sounds right. This should help them to choose the right tense.

Rescue!   *(NLS: Y2 T2 S5)*